HOW TO P.A.R.E.N.T.
(Possibly Actually Remember Everything Next Time)

Copyright © 2023 Jacqueline Santillan

How to P.A.R.E.N.T. (Possibly Remember Everything Next Time)

ISBN-13 9798396783737

All rights reserved. This book or any portion thereof may not be reproduced or used in any manner whatsoever without the express written permission of the publisher except for the use of brief quotations in a book review.

jackie@kindmindssmarthearts.com

HOW TO P.A.R.E.N.T.
(Possibly Actually Remember Everything Next Time)

Tips and Tricks to Help you Remember Parenting Tips and Tricks

Jackie Santillan

For my Maximoo

I love you to Timbukten and back again;

So muchy much

The mosty most from coast to coast.

Preface

If there is one thing that unites all parents, it's the admission that this job ain't easy. There is so much to do to keep our kids alive every day. There are so many lessons to teach. We are always worried that we are damaging our kids in some way (and we are - no matter how wonderfully we do things). On top of all that, we have a million other responsibilities and our own trauma to process. It is, as they say, a lot.

We are part of a generation that wants to be intentional in our parenting, but we have very few examples of how to do so. Our parents didn't model respectful parenting techniques for us, and the concepts are not always intuitive. There are many helpful books on the topic of gentle/respectful/conscious/intentional parenting (and I'll include a resource list) but researching can be overwhelming! I highly recommend getting audio books and consuming the books while cooking, driving, or doing chores.

      Even if you do take the time to read or listen to a book about parenting, there is so much information that it is usually incredibly difficult to remember or implement in a stressful situation. Throughout my life, I have always created little acronyms and mnemonics to help myself remember anything: where I parked the car, the code for a gate, and the names of the Great Lakes (S&M Hurts Every One: Superior, Michigan, Huron, Eerie, Ontario- there's a freebie for you!). And just so you know, this is most definitely a compilation of things I have learned. I didn't invent gentle or respectful parenting, but it has completely changed my life and the lives of people to whom I recommend it. And anything that can make implementing it an easier process is a worthwhile venture, IMO.

The purpose of this book, is to give you easy-to-remember strategies for different parenting challenges. Each chapter will start with a mnemonic of some sort, sprinkle in some explanation, and then end with some sample scripts you could use with your kids if necessary. I'll attempt to address multiple age groups, but please know you can tweak any of the scripts to fit your child's age.

And, I welcome any questions via email if you can't think of an example of a logical consequence, or you need help adjusting the wording, or you have a cute example of your kids doing something or WHATEVER. Feel free to slide into my dms on Instagram or email me at the address at the end of this book. I really do love answering your questions when I can.

Thank you so much for trusting me enough to help you with your most special things: your kids. I promise to help as much as I can with the knowledge I have. And I promise to keep learning and creating for you as long as it makes sense for us all.

Please enjoy. I hope it's so helpful.

Jackie xo

Table of Contents

Part I: But, like, why?.. 1

Part II: Acronyms

1. **HOW** to Teach Your Child Expectations for New Situations...................... 23
2. **8C**: How to Communicate Your Expectations at Home............................ 31
3. **The BRATT Method:** What to Do When Your Child Flips Out 41
4. **Giving Your Kids SPACE:** When They Aren't Quite Ready to Use Calm Down Strategies.. 51
5. **Help Your Kids to get ALONG:** Conflict Resolution Strategies................ 59
6. **OOPS! They Did it Again:** Teaching Your Kids to Apologize................... 67
7. **STOP!** Stopping Kids From Hitting (And Other Aggressive Behaviors)....... 72
8. **ALTS:** Alternatives (or Choices)..79
9. **DO IT!** When You Have to Get Your Kids Ready, Like Now..................... 85
10. **WHY** are they doing that thing, AGAIN? 91
11. **THE ABCs:** Helping Your Kids Clean Their Rooms..................................98
12. **TRAUMA:** How We Can Support Our Kids Through Tough Times 105
13. **The 4Hs:** How to Be There for Your Kid..111
14. **HOTT:** How to Figure Out Why Your Kids Are Struggling (or are feeling Hott)..118
15. **WHOA:** How to Respond to Shocking Expressions 124

Part III: The Other Important Stuff

16. **The Nurse and the Narrator:** What to Do With More Than One Child 131
17. **Emotional Regulation:** The Steps, The Signs, The Strategies 136
18. **Songs & Mantras**..153
19. **Recommendations and Resources**..160

References..163
Acknowledgements..165

Part I:
But, Like, Why?

If you are reading this book, likely one of four scenarios is happening. The first is that you are 6 months pregnant and someone gifted it to you at your baby shower. You have piles of muslin blankets and wipe warmers and various other baby accoutrement taking up every space in your home. You are opening boxes, decorating, going to doctor's appointments, and generally freaking out about the idea that soon a little dinky doozie is going to take over your lives. You smiled, said "thank you" (probably even wrote a thank you note), and shoved the book into a basket in your bathroom which you *promised* you would dive into whilst pooping. But we all know you are just going to bring your phone in the bathroom. We all know you aren't going to read this book while pregnant. And that's fine. Just don't throw it away. Keep it in your nursery and pull it out while you are doing those nighttime feeds. Read it aloud to your child at bedtime the first year of their life. They won't know what you're talking about anyway. Maybe they'll even absorb some emotional regulation skills by osmosis.

    The second option is that you have a 4-16 month old baby at home who is just an absolute delight. You can't get enough snuggles and kissies. But last weekend you went to your friend's house and you witnessed their 5-year-old kid refuse to come inside from the backyard by throwing their entire body into a mud pit and clinging to a tree root; or you went to Olive Garden and saw a 3-year-old have a complete screaming meltdown because the breadstick was "too bready." Of course, you could never imagine your darling baby angel doing something like that, but you can never be too careful. You think it might behoove you to do some light research into understanding children's behavior.

The third possibility is that you are noticing it is becoming increasingly difficult to communicate with your child as they have started walking, talking, and forming their own opinions. Just as preparing for a wedding seems to disregard the notion that you will actually have to be a married couple afterwards; having a baby can seem like the end of the process when, in fact, it's just the start. You want to address these issues head-on, and you are looking for ideas. Most likely a friend recommended this book (or my social media content) to you.

And lastly, you are maybe a friend or family member of mine and I am shamelessly using this as a gift for your birthday or some other gift-giving situation. It was either this or a personalized t-shirt I made with my vinyl-cutting machine. At least you can regift this. You're welcome.

Regardless of your reason, I am glad and grateful that you are here. I hope to provide you easy to remember ways to help strengthen the connection and trust between you and your child, and to help you raise a child who is happy, emotionally intelligent, resilient, and able to problem solve.

Here's the thing. We are all parenting the only way we know how. Unlike driving a car, we aren't taught and tested before being entrusted with the life of a child. We are expected; as animals I suppose, to know how to do it. Unless we have taken classes, we all do what comes naturally to us. That generally comes from observing our parents and other adult figures during our own childhoods, and replicating what they did to us with our children. We do it without even meaning to. And that's why modeling behaviors *with intention* is so important. Our kids are going to do what they see us do when they are children and as they grow into adults. If we want to break cycles that are harmful, traumatic, or just not evidence-based best practices, it's going to take work and intentionality.

Breaking Cycles Ain't For The Faint of Heart

One of the hardest parts of parenting; and definitely the part that you don't expect, is the fact that you will be revisiting so many parts of your own childhood. You'll understand your parents and their motivations in ways you never could have otherwise. You'll realize they were just young people making impossible decisions without any training and hoping for the best. You'll question their reasons for doing other things in certain ways. You'll think, "As a parent, I would never dream of doing it that way." And more than likely, you'll make a conscious choice to follow in their footsteps or create a new parenting path.

And once you begin exploring different parenting styles and the impact each one can have on a child, you won't be able to unsee it. It may be hard to accept. It will be difficult to implement. It might be the biggest challenge you face in your adult life, but once you know better, you will want to do better. When someone says, "I was spanked and I turned out fine," you'll think, "But did you?". When another person says, "I do it this way, because I'm old school," you may even shudder a little.

I've used this analogy before, so if you've heard it, feel free to skip a paragraph or two. Consider the "old school" car seat. It was basically a flat surface for the baby to sit on with a t-shaped metal bar in front to secure them. I've seen a carton of eggs transported with more care these days. After hundreds of car accidents; in which children were maimed or worse, the standards for car seat safety changed. Currently, a car seat has a 5-point harness, an angle indicator, a head support, and various other requirements in order to comply with safety regulations. Once we had the evidence to support the idea that a modified crab-fishing cage wasn't sufficient to protect our children in the event that our giant tin cans on wheels collide with a tree at 60 mph, we altered the design (and we continue to revise it) to improve our children's chances for survival in a car accident.

      We have evidence, data, facts, and proof that old-school-do-what-I-say-right-now-because-I-said-so-or-you'll-get-the-belt parenting is damaging to our kids. In fact, spanking has been found to create the same level of brain trauma as more violent forms of abuse (*Anderson, 2021*). Many countries have banned corporal punishment; making it illegal. The American Academy of Pediatrics does not recommend spanking, but as of now, it is not illegal in the United States. Studies have shown that; although physical and fear-based methods of discipline may be effective in the short term, the long term effects on mental health and impacts on the parent/child relationship are negative (*Howard, 2018*). Spanking affects the brain in the same way that more violent forms of physical abuse do; causing children to live in a state of fight or flight more often than is healthy.

Parenting Styles

Depending on how you were raised and what you've since learned, you will likely adopt one of the four major parenting styles. Although, if you're like me, there will be days where you'll find yourself shifting from one to another. Days without sleep and coffee, days of mental instability, days of sickness- all of these can lead to a less effective parenting situation. And that's okay. I know I am doing my best, and I know you are too. If we make a mistake, the best thing we can do is apologize to our kids and do better the next time. They will learn so much from our apologies. We are human. We make mistakes. We learn from our mistakes. These are all things that will be better taught through observation. So, make those mistakes. Our kids need to see us be less than perfect and take accountability. (Again, they're learning by watching us just as you learned from watching your parents).

When I say there will be days that I will be less effective, I usually mean that I have strayed from my preferred parenting style: authoritative/gentle/conscious. Dang, I wish there was a better name for it. Whatever IT is, it has been proven to be the one that most usually results in happy, well-adjusted kids. It is also the most draining for the parent. It requires a lot of mental energy and a lot of stamina. So, just as an effective workout trainer wouldn't recommend that a person push their body to the physical limit every day, I want to remind you that it would be dangerous for you to assume you could push yourself to your mental limit every day. It's okay to be less than perfect.

There are four basic parenting styles. I won't go into too much detail about them, because that's definitely not why you're here. I just want you to have a basic understanding of where you are so you can decide where you want to go (*Morin, 2022; Mullins & Tashjian, 2023*).

Uninvolved: The uninvolved parent is "hands-off." They tend to let children do as they please and don't know too much about what is going on in their children's lives. This is not because they don't love their children. Most frequently, it's because they don't know how to do anything else. Parenting is overwhelming. Or it could also be that their careers and lives are too demanding and they feel that they don't have the time to invest in their children. Children raised by uninvolved parents tend to lack coping skills and self-esteem. They also struggle with depression and may act out in school as a way to get attention.

Permissive: The permissive parent, as the name suggests, allows the child to be in charge. They are usually very loving, but struggle to set boundaries and expectations for their children. Children raised by permissive parents tend to have trouble developing good habits academically and physically. They may struggle at school and have poor hygiene. They can be bossy and demanding of others.

Authoritarian: The authoritarian parent is the parent who thinks kids should obey their parents without question. They lean very heavily on control, fear, and punishment to discipline and guide their children. Children raised by authoritarian parents tend to have self-esteem issues because their suggestions and ideas have been ignored. They can be sneaky because they have learned to hide any behaviors that they know an authority figure wouldn't approve of. They can grow to be hostile and/or depressed and anxious.

Authoritative*: The authoritative parent allows their children to have a voice in their home while maintaining boundaries and expectations. It is in the same category as gentle or conscious parenting. Since there is no definitive set of guidelines for this style, concepts can vary from coach to proponent to expert. But they all rely on the principles of compassion, connection, boundaries, and expectations while allowing children to express their thoughts and concerns. The techniques in this book are all derived from this method of parenting. Children raised by authoritative parents tend to lead the pack in happiness, success, maturity, and assertiveness. It is evidence-based best practice in parenting (*Morin, 2022; Mullins & Tashjian, 2023*).

*Can I just say it drives me bananas that first we have the term "gentle parenting," which makes everyone think we are letting kids do whatever they want. And THEN there is the similarity between authoritarian and authoritative which can only lead to misunderstandings? Who do I contact about this? Is there a supervisor?

My Own Experience

I could (and probably will) write an entire book about my path to becoming a gentle parent, but here's a little overview. Although my mom led with compassion and connection early in my life, she later became a permissive parent for my elementary and middle school years and then an uninvolved parent in my high school life.

As a middle schooler, my mom would try to ground me- which meant sending me to my room where I had my own TV and phone line (it was the 90s). I would come out of my room an hour later and say, "Can I be ungrounded now?" And she always said, "yes." I'm sure it was partially because she didn't have the strength to keep enforcing the consequence, but it could have also been partially because she felt guilty for how she'd handled the preceding conversation. My mom's cycle was rage and regret. And throughout my life, she'd yell at me and then apologize.

When I was in high school, the situation was worse. My mom rarely knew where I was. I would sometimes have boys stay the night at the house. I would smoke cigarettes and other things in my room, and she would say nothing of it. Of course, she was battling her own demons at the time. My dad had moved to Malaysia when I was 11, leaving her with two little rascals to take care of on her own. He then married someone 9 years older than me and started another family with her. This was just a few years after my mom had battled non-Hodgkins lymphoma and subsequently was committed to a mental health facility for schizo-affective and bipolar disorders after attempting to die by suicide. That, on top of her alcohol and cocaine addictions, put her in no position to care for two children; and she withdrew to her bedroom.

I tell you all of this not to garner sympathy, but to prove that no matter what you were shown as a child, you have the ability to break cycles. You have the ability to learn and do better than what was shown to you by your parents. Oh, and I wanted to share also that the thing that saved me through all of this was love. I KNEW my mom and my dad loved me even though they were incapable of raising me in the way I needed. So, if you're letting your children know you love them, that will do more than you know.

Because my home life was so unpredictable, I felt the most safe at school. That's not to say I liked school. In fact, I spent a great deal of my time trying to figure out how to stay home from school. School was boring to me; perhaps because it felt so routine and predictable, but also because I was pretty smart. A lot of school could have been an email, in my opinion (but this was before email was a thing).

When I graduated University of Texas at Austin with a Bachelor's degree in English Literature, I was somehow shocked I couldn't find a job. (Who wouldn't want to hire a 22-year-old who read Shakespeare and wore tank tops to job interviews?). After about 6 months of searching, I decided to start substitute teaching and get my alternative teaching certification. School had always been my safe place. I assumed this would be easy.

It was not easy. I had very little training in how to manage a classroom, so I was unable to teach anything. I spent my days yelling at students and my nights developing a pretty healthy drinking problem and crying. I was put on a growth plan my first year teaching and cried in my principal's office; telling her, "You don't understand. I'm Jackie Cottle. I don't fail." My ego would not allow me to ask for help, and to be honest, I wasn't even sure what help I needed.

And then I attended a CHAMPs training. It was a course designed to give teachers a framework for setting expectations in their classrooms, and my LIFE CHANGED. My kids knew what I expected of them. They were usually willing to do it. The crying, yelling, and drinking decreased drastically. My kids were learning. I felt confident. Things were improving. I went to more trainings. I learned how to build relationships with my kids through programs like Love and Logic, Capturing Kids Hearts, and Conscious Discipline. I even became a mentor teacher after a few years of honing my skills. Teachers were watching little old me, the failure, to see how to do it.

I decided to get my master's degree in school counseling. I finished the program, and then I got pregnant. I'll never say never, but I doubt I'll get to use my degree in a school setting. I could never have known how all of these steps would lead me to be a better mother. I am so grateful to have had all of these experiences before having a baby. I wish we lived in a world where more parents had access to the knowledge I gained in those years teaching and learning. But wait. We do. God bless TikTok.

Okay, We Get It. Let's Get Started.

And one more thing before we start with all the tips and tricks that are going to change everything about your children's behavior: these tips and tricks are not going to change everything about your children's behavior. Not every idea will work every time with every child in every situation on every day.

Think of this book as something similar to a car toolkit- the jumper cables, car jack, and Fix-a-Flat your parents gave you when you got your first car. You will have the basics, but there is a possibility you may need to seek out more specific tools for specific issues (I'll list some resources at the end and you can check out some of the references for additional information). You may even need to hire a mechanic if things get too difficult to repair with your "cars." And there is no shame in that. You wouldn't feel bad hiring a professional to replace your carburetor, so don't feel bad for involving a professional if that's what you need to help your child. If you approach difficult situations with your kids with the curiosity of a mechanic hearing a rattle in the engine, you'll learn more about what they need and how to be there for them.

That said, these mnemonics should make it helpful for you to recall some things in those heated moments where your brain is not functioning at full capacity. And they are a good place to start.

Part II
Acronyms

CHAPTER 1

HOW

How to Teach Your Child Your Expectations for New Situations

(or really how to remind them of your expectations anywhere)

The Basics:

H - Help; how do they get help or attention from you?

O - Volume Knob (think of the 'O' as the knob or remember "Output")

W - What should they do with their body?

The Thought Process:

As an adult, you have most likely been to countless new buildings and outdoor places. You have interacted with people in professional settings, school settings, legal settings, and party settings. You have been to funerals, courtrooms, movie theaters, malls, restaurants, airports, buses, taxis, etc. You have either been explicitly taught how to behave in those places or you have learned from social cues over the years.

Your child is walking into each of these situations as if they are walking onto a new planet in a new galaxy. They know nothing about what they are seeing as far as people, decorations, doors, furniture, machines; and it is all very, very interesting. They also know nothing about what the people in these places are expecting to see from a "well-behaved" child in these situations. Yet we hear parents say all the time, "Why are you doing that? You should know better!"

Firstly, kids probably can't articulate why they are doing it other than "it's new and interesting and I'm curious." And secondly, how could they possibly know better– unless you have told them.

Telling your child your expectations before entering a new setting can help alleviate their anxiety and set them up for success. Think about they first day of school when you were younger. You didn't know where your classrooms were, you didn't know who your teachers were or what they would expect, and you didn't know who would be in your classes. On day one, you were probably a little buzzing ball of nerves and anxiety. By day two, you already knew the drill. You knew what to expect. You felt safer. The part of your brain that controls your fight or flight tendencies had passed on its responsibilities to other parts, and you were able to enjoy yourself more because you felt safer. You were able to learn because you felt safer. Kids (and adults) thrive with knowledge, consistency, and safety (*Central, Churchill, Tyner & Pondiscio, 2021*).

Once you've told your kids what you expect, will you have to remind them of your expectations at some point? Most likely. But there are fewer chances for them to be confused about what you want if you directly tell them what you want.

How it Works:

Before you go anywhere, *think* about what you expect from your child. Tell them at least two times before entering the new situation. You could tell them once in the car on the way there, and once right before you go in the door. If they are comfortable with eye contact, make sure they are looking at you when you explain it so there is less chance for confusion.

In as many words as your child needs to understand your intentions, tell them exactly what you expect. You can ask them to repeat it back in their own words to make sure they have understood. And you can honestly do this every time you switch to a different activity during the day. Even if your child has been to the movies before, a quick refresher before going in wouldn't hurt.

If you notice your child struggling to remember your expectations after you've given them twice, YOU CAN REMIND THEM. It's okay for kids to need support. We get support all the time- we get to hear the safety precautions every time we fly, we hear and snooze our alarms repeatedly, and Netflix asks us over and over if we're still watching. And if hearing the reminders isn't enough, you can come up with hand signals that communicate different things. We've all "zipped our lips" before, right? You could also make a little sticky note or card with images and/or words for your child to carry with them in the store. Holding onto something will sort of force you to think about it every now and then.

Some Sample Scripts:

Going to the grocery store

Sweetheart, we are going to the grocery store. When we get there…

H: If you need help, just say "Mom" one time. I'll answer as soon as I can.

O: Use an indoor voice*

W: You can either walk close enough so that I could touch you, or you can sit in the cart. Keep your hands to yourself. You may pick one thing, and that is the only thing you should touch.

*make sure you have practiced "indoor voices" before you go to the store.

Going to the movies

Hey Dude, we're going to see a movie today. While we're in the theater…

H: If you need my attention or you need the restroom, you can tap my shoulder and I'll lean over to you.

O: While the movie is playing, you should be silent. If you need attention, whisper in my ear after I lean to you.

W: Sit still in your chair and only touch your fidget spinner or your snack.

Going to the playground

Let's get ready for the park! While we're there…

H: If you need me, run over to me to ask or just shout my name if you're hurt.

O: You can use your loud voice as long as you don't bother anyone.

W: When we get out of the car, stay with me until I can watch you. You can play on the playground, in the grass, or on the basketball court, but let me know first if you move to a new location.

With a child who needs minimal words at a play date

H: If you need me, say, "Mama.'

O: quiet voices

W: soft touch

CHAPTER 2

The 8C Method

How to Communicate Your Expectations or Rules at Home

The Basics:

1. **Calm & Close**
2. **Connect & Communicate**
3. **Chance & Consequence**
4. **Carry out Consistently**

The Thought Process

    I have yet to meet a child that ALWAYS does what their parent asks them to do the first time EVERY time. Heck, I haven't met an adult who can do that. Think about the fact that every time you drive, you see a speed limit sign telling you how fast to go. And, if you're anything like me, you drive five to seven miles over that limit. It's the limit! We aren't supposed to pass it at all, and we go above it. There are potential consequences for us too: speeding tickets, car accidents, loss of our driving privileges, and even jail time if we do it habitually. Yet, we still do it. Why do we expect our children to be able to hear our expectations once and follow them perfectly?

It's unlikely they will be able to make the right choice every time, but it is possible to help them understand that you have expectations that should be followed. If you received a speeding ticket each time the needle barely surpassed the limit, you'd probably learn a little bit more quickly.

Just as you communicate your expectations to your child while you are out and about by telling them HOW to behave, you will need to explicitly do so in your home. It's likely that there will be boundaries and limits your child will push over and over again. This method is great for being specific about what you will and will not allow, and for enforcing your limits once you have set them. If you follow the steps, your child will quickly learn that you are not going to let them "get away with" whatever undesirable behavior they are displaying.

And here's a brief overview of natural and logical consequences as you might use them on step three. A **natural consequence** is a consequence that will happen whether or not you intervene because of your child's actions. You will not have to do anything for these to take place and they are frequently the most effective because they are the ones your child will likely experience in life. A **logical consequence** is different than a punishment because of the intention behind it. A logical consequence has the goal of teaching your child something that will help them to become a better human. **Punishment** typically comes from the desire to control a child. It is designed to guilt, shame, hurt, or prove that the parent must be obeyed because they are the authority figure. In order to be different from punishments, **logical consequences** should be **related** to the behavior, **reasonable**, and done **respectfully** (*Team, 2022*).

(Also, if you'd like a song to help you remember the steps in a shorter way, check out the song chapter at the end of the book).

Here are some examples:

Situation or Behavior	Natural Consequence	Logical Consequence	Punishment
Child refuses to pick up toys outside	Toys get rusty in the rain or run over by a car	Parent puts toys away in an unreachable place for a short time and reteaches child how to care for toys before they can use them again	Parent throws away all child's toys or breaks them intentionally in front of child
Child hits another child	Kids don't want to play with hitting child	Parent separates children. Hurt child is attended to first and given something to play with independently. Child who hit has conversation with parent about anger and how to resolve it in the future. Child cannot play with the other one until they have mastered a calm down strategy.	Child who hit the other child gets spanked
Child doesn't	Child gets a bad	Parent talks to	Child is

| do homework | grade for homework and doesn't get to practice material | child about why they are struggling to complete homework. If schedule is too full, maybe something has to give. If it's too difficult, maybe they need a tutor. | grounded for a month. |

How it Works:

If and when your child does something that you do not want them to do, follow these steps.

1. Get **calm** and get **close.** Whatever you need to do to calm yourself down before helping your child is fine. You are the adult and you will be modeling the acceptable tone. I will often take a deep breath and close my eyes for a moment. Sometimes, I will even leave the room (assuming it's safe) and

do a quick silent scream or butterfly taps. Whatever it takes. Then, once you are calm, walk over to your child.

2. **Connect** with your child by physically getting down to their level if possible. If you stand above them with your hands on your hips, you may communicate anger and aggression. Try to be softer and lower with your pose to communicate a willingness to work together. Make eye contact and hold their hands if it is comfortable for both of you. If it is not, you could put your hand on their shoulder or simply stand nearby. Directly and specifically **communicate** your expectation.

3. Give them a **chance** to comply. Really try to let them do it. If they cannot, then tell them the logical **consequence*** for the next time it happens.

4. The very next time (and any other time) they do the thing, **consistently carry out** the consequence.

Some Sample Scripts:

Jumping on the couch

1. Calm & Close: Take a deep breath. Walk to your child.
2. Connect & Communicate: Squat down and make eye contact. Say, "It seems like you're having fun burning energy by jumping. The couch is for sitting and lying down. You can jump on your trampoline."
3. Chance & Consequence: Give them a chance. If they do it again, say, "Oops. Looks like you jumped again. The next time you jump, you'll have to go play in another room."
4. Consistently Carry out: If it happens, walk with them to another room to play and get them started

Touching a sibling's toy

1. Calm & Close: Splash cold water on your face. Walk to your child.

2. Connect & Communicate: Make eye contact. Say, "You were hoping to play with the blocks with your brother. He has been working hard to build that, and he doesn't want you to touch it. Please only touch blocks that you have picked for yourself."
3. Chance & Consequence: Give them a chance. If they do it again, say, "Oh dear. Looks like you touched his tower again. The next time you do it, you'll have to come hang out with me in the kitchen."
4. Consistently Carry out: If it happens, bring them to the kitchen table to draw or play blocks instead.

Playing with a ball in the house

1. Calm & Close: Close your eyes. Count to 5. Walk to your child.
2. Connect & Communicate: Sit down and make eye contact. Say, "You can play with the ball outside. The house is not an okay place to play with the ball."

3. Chance & Consequence: Give them a chance. If they do it again, say, "Uh-oh. You bounced the ball in the house again. The next time you do that, I am going to put it somewhere else until tomorrow*."
4. Consistently Carry out: If it happens, put the ball away until the next day.

*Throwing the ball away is not an appropriate consequence. The time for which you take away a toy will be different for different ages. A toddler might only need 5-10 minutes without the toy to learn the lesson.

Chapter 3

The BRATT Method

What to Do When Your Child Flips Out

(Or more accurately, has a tantrum)

The Basics:

B - Breathe (or calm down)

R - Recognize what is physically happening

A - Acknowledge and validate their emotions

T - Tame the tantrum

T - Teach what to do next time

The Thought Process:

You know when your internet goes out and you have to call your service provider? You have to answer seemingly endless riddles from the customer service robot before they will even connect you to a human. At some point, you shout, "REPRESENTATIVE!" and refuse to say anything else until robo-helper is crying in a corner, and you are finally speaking to someone who is in the wrong department. And then when they say they are going to connect you to someone in the correct department, the call drops and you have to start the whole process over again, so you decide you don't need internet anymore and you're just going to live in a tent on a mountainside? No? Just me?

    Whenever I call customer service, I have the potential to lose my cool. It hits on some of my biggest triggers: I feel like my time is being wasted, and I feel like I am being regarded as stupid. The thing is, I could go into it prepared. I KNOW this about myself, and I am still unable to calm down sometimes. I can also notice the feelings showing up in my body, and sometimes I can't stop myself to take a deep breath. I am always so proud of myself when I make it through a call without saying anything that I will replay in my head as I try to fall asleep later.

Everybody gets frustrated and loses their cool sometimes. It doesn't matter if you're the best parent. It doesn't matter if you have the most amazing children. Kids (and grown-ups) are going to have tantrums and most likely meltdowns too. No adult has the ability to maintain composure at all times, so how can we expect that from our kids? Calming yourself down in the face of a tantrum requires having the ability to recognize that a big feeling is coming, remembering the strategies you've learned to calm down, and choosing to use one of them. That's really hard to handle for an adult with a fully developed prefrontal lobe. It's damn-near impossible for a child who is still learning emotional regulation strategies.

The best part about talking to your kids about their physical and emotional reactions with the BRATT method, is that they will begin to identify them in themselves and be able to catch themselves (sometimes) with your help before they tantrum gets too intense. The worst part is that they will start to tell you when you have forgotten to self-regulate as well. My son will say to me, "Mama, you raised your voice when you were angry. You should have taken a deep breath to calm down." And he's not wrong. It's just tough when a 3-year-old calls you out.

Note: If your child is over the age of 4 and having frequent or intense tantrums, you may want to contact your physician or a mental health professional to ensure there are no underlying concerns.

How it Works:

If your child is in the middle of a tantrum or is whining and arguing with you, follow these steps. (And just FYI, this won't work if your child is in a meltdown. I'll talk more about meltdowns in the chapter called SPACE. If your child is "unreachable" because they are screaming or crying, you won't be able to reason with them. They will need space first.)

1. Breathe. When I say "breathe" here, I am using it as a short form for whatever strategies you use to calm yourself down. This is not a time to tell your child to breathe because that will likely make them more angry or emotional. Rather, this is your opportunity to regulate your own emotions, so that you'll be able to respond to your child calmly. It's also a great chance to model calm down strategies for your kids. If they see you take a deep breath, and see that it works for you, it's likely they will try that technique.

Some other ideas to self-regulate:

-splash cold water on your face

-run cold water on your wrist

-count backwards from 5

-close your eyes

-repeat a mantra

-walk away for a minute

-cross your arms on your chest and tap rhythmically as you breathe deeply

2. Recognize: Say out loud what your child is doing with their face, body, and other objects around them. They may be so caught up that they don't realize what is happening and this can help bring their attention to what they are doing.

3. Acknowledge: Notice and validate their feelings. How many times have we heard kids say that "parents don't understand." Sometimes just saying what you think they are feeling will show them that you do understand, and sometimes you'll be wrong. If that's the case, they will usually tell you. Frequently, feeling heard and understood is enough to calm them down.

4. Tame: Offer them suggestions for calming down. You might verbally remind them of some of the calming techniques you have practiced with them ahead of time. You might just hand them a stuffed animal or point to their calm down corner. In the heat of the moment, they might forget what they know how to do, and you can gently remind them without forcing them to try it. Sometimes a good cry is all they need. In this step, sometimes the best way to tame the problem will be to

offer a replacement activity or item until there is a better time to address the big emotion.

5. Teach: Later on, when everyone is calm, teach them what to do next time. You can revisit the calm down corner and show them how to use the tools. You could role play with them or have them draw a picture of how things should go next time. You could even give them a script to know how to appropriately say what they want in the future.

Some Sample Scripts:

When your child takes something from another child

Breathe: Take a deep breath

Recognize: Walk to the child. Get down on their level. Say, "You took that car out of your brother's hand. He is crying."

Acknowledge: Say, "It seems like you wanted that car, and you didn't know how to ask for it. That must have been frustrating."

Tame: Help him to give the car back to the other child and suggest that he uses another car or another toy in the meantime.

Teach: When both children have stopped crying and are relatively calm, you can remind the snatcher that he took a car without asking, and ask if he would like to apologize. You can also say, "Next time you would like to use a car, say to your brother, 'I'd like to use that car when you're finished,' and then do something else until he is done."

When your child doesn't want to leave the park

Breathe: close your eyes, take a breath, say to yourself, "They aren't giving me a hard time. They are having a hard time."

Recognize: Walk to the child. Get down on their level. Say, "You are hiding behind the slide and crying. It seems like you don't feel ready to leave the park."

Acknowledge: Say, "You were having a great time, and now it's time to go. It's really hard to stop when you're having fun." (Make sure you say this sincerely; otherwise it can come off as sarcastic or patronizing).

Tame: Say, "Let's make the way back to the car fun too. Do you want to race or tip toe like little mice over there?"

Teach: Later on, when everyone is calm, discuss the situation again. You could say, "It was really hard for you to leave the park today. What can I do to help you next time? Did you like racing to the car? Would you like me to give you a countdown or set a timer?" You can also teach some calm down strategies to use out in public like deep breaths, squeezing their body tight and then releasing, or closing their eyes and counting backwards.

Chapter 4

Giving Your Kids SPACE

When They Aren't Quite Ready to Use Calm Down Strategies

The Basics:

S - Sit near them

P - Put your hand out or offer connection

A - Accept any emotional displays

C - Calm yourself down and model strategies

E - Expect that it will take longer than you think

The Thought Process:

At this point, you're probably thinking, "Okay. Sure. I can talk to my kid when they are able to listen, but there are some times when it seems like they can't even hear me." And, yes. You're right. There is a difference between a tantrum (where your child is still working from the part of their brain that allows them to reason with you) and a meltdown (where your child is seemingly unreachable because they are functioning in the brainstem). They are either completely overstimulated, over-tired, hungry, or in fight-or-flight mode and you won't be able to use the BRATT method with them yet. First, you'll need to get them to a relative level of calm that is approachable. And one way to do this is to offer and/or give them space.

How it Works:

You will know when your child is having a meltdown. They are screaming, they are red, they are crying, they can't hear you, etc… If this is the case, you can either offer them space or just give it to them (and let them know you are doing so. "I'll be in the hallway when you're ready." They actually can hear you a little). And then,

S – Sit near them. You don't have to be in the same room, but be somewhere that they can easily access you if they need to. Ideally, you won't start doing anything else while you are doing this (i.e., don't start doing dishes or scrolling on Instagram). The goal is for them to know you are physically there with them in empathy during this big emotion.

P – Put out your hand or offer connection. You can ask if they would like a hug. You can hold out a stuffy they love. You can just offer your hand and see if they take it. You could even just make eye contact (unless they aren't ready for it yet). Indicate physically that your intention is connection.

A – Accept any* emotional displays. If your child cries, let them cry. If your child sticks their tongue out, let them. If they need to flop around on the floor safely-ish, so be it. You might even feel comfortable with them throwing or hitting things.

*as long as none of these actions are dangerous to themselves, you, or others

C – Calm yourself down and model calm down strategies. This is especially helpful if you've practiced these strategies beforehand. You will need to be calm yourself, anyway. There is no way you will be able to help your child emotionally regulate if you aren't regulated, but it's also extremely helpful to remind your child without verbally saying anything in these moments. They will need your guidance, but won't be able to focus on your words. Seeing you effectively calm down should be extremely beneficial.

E – Expect that this will take longer than you would like. I know you told your parents you would be at that restaurant in 20 minutes and you don't have time for this. If you try to force your child to calm down, it will take longer. Or worse, if you frighten your child into compliance, it may cause them to dismiss their own emotions later in life.

A Sample Situation:

You are late for a doctor's appointment and your child won't put on their shoes. It started as a tantrum; a way for them to avoid going to the appointment, but then you lost your cool. You were frustrated that you were going to be late. Now they are scared and now feel like they are in trouble with the person who is usually their safety net. So, they have escalated to a meltdown. They are screaming. They can't hear a word you are saying. They are red in the face and crying.

S - Sit on the ground near them, but don't add any more stimulation. Don't try to have a conversation. Don't try to make eye contact. Don't try to hug them. You could say something like, "I'm going to give you some space, but I'm here if you need me."

P - Put out your hand or offer connection once they are able to make eye contact with you. You know your kid better than I do. Sometimes, mine will scoot on the floor to hold my hand. Sometimes, he will run/crawl for a big hug and I will rock him. Sometimes, I can just make a silly face and he will laugh. Connect so they know you still love them even when their feelings get out of control.

A - Accept the crying, the screaming, the kicking; as long as they aren't a danger to themselves or anyone else. Try to avoid telling them to stop, and don't give them "rewards" like candy or bribes to get it to stop. If one of their calm down strategies is to hug a stuffy, you could hand them their stuffy.

C - Calm yourself and model calm down strategies. Without making it cartoonish, take some exaggerated deep breaths so they can see you calming down. You could also hug a stuffy or put your face on a cool surface.

E - Expect that this is going to take time. You might already be late, and that stinks. If you don't stop to help your child through this, they will either have repeated meltdowns for the rest of the day, or they will learn to suppress their big emotions to keep you happy. While this may seem like it's an easier way to keep the peace, suppressing emotions can lead to bigger outbursts with bigger kids down the road.

Chapter 5

Help Your Kids to get ALONG*

Conflict Resolution Strategies

The Basics:

A - Ask if they would like help

L - Listen to both sides without judgement

O - Offer your understanding of their feelings

N - Name some possible solutions

G - Guide them to make a choice

The Thought Process:

      Once upon a time I was a teacher. Beyond being a teacher, I was also a teacher mentor, and one year, my mentee and I did not get along. I mean, I was supposed to be helping him, and our personalities and opinions clashed so much that we had to walk away from multiple conversations. Normally, I am the type of person to avoid conflict, but ESPECIALLY as a supervisor of sorts, I knew I had to involve a mediator. It was not okay to leave those conversations unfinished; unresolved. Even as an adult, there are times that we might need help communicating with another person. Imagine how tricky these conversations could be for our kids.

This chapter comes with a built-in footnote: *it's best to let your kids try to work out their conflicts on their own. However, none of us are born knowing how to resolve conflict. You stepping in and helping them through the process from time-to-time will help them to understand how to navigate a difficult conversation.

I can't tell you a definite moment to step in, but maybe if you see tufts of hair flying or hear sounds louder than 10 decibels coming from the living room. I kid. If you hear that things are getting too heated or are becoming physical, it would be a great time to step in and help.

How it Works:

If you notice that your children (or your child and their friend) are "activated," walk to them and get down to their level. They will already be upset, so you towering over them will come off as aggressive. Make sure they know your goal is to help by connecting, making eye contact, and staying calm.

A - Ask if they actually want help. If they think they can resolve it (without violence) and say so, feel free to turn around and leave at this point.

L - Listen to both sides. If they say they'd like help, explain that each of them will get a turn to talk. Each gets to explain, and then each gets to respond. And listen to them both talk without trying to decide who is right. You just want the facts.

O - Offer your understanding of their feelings. Repeating their concerns in your own words will help them to feel heard. It will also possibly help them to understand each other's perspectives. If they hear it from your mouth, it might not be as hurtful or anger-inducing.

N – Name possible solutions. Encourage each person to name 1-2 solutions. If they struggle to come up with anything, you could get the ball rolling with some ideas for compromise. You'll often be surprised at how many great options they come up with.

G – Guide them to make a choice; and "guide" is the operative word. Let them make the choice but help them to understand what might happen if that's the choice they make. Once they make it, congratulate them on making a compromise. It can be so hard.

Some Sample Scripts:

If your kids are fighting over a toy

A – Calmly walk to your kids and say, "It seems like you guys are having a hard time with the Bluey action figures. Would you like some help?"

L – If they say yes, listen to both sides.

> 5 yo: I was playing with it first. He grabbed it out of my hand without asking.

> 3 yo: He always gets to play with Bluey and he makes me play with Bingo. I want to play with Bluey once.

O – Offer your understanding. "It seems like [5] had the toy first and is upset because [3] grabbed it from him. [3] it seems like you're upset because you feel like you don't get to play with the action figure you like best. Is that right?

N – If they confirm that you are correct, help them to come up with options.

> You: What are some things we could do to resolve this?

> 5yo: We could take turns.

3yo: He could just give it to me.

5yo: You could ask me before you take something.

3yo: I could play with something else.

5yo: We could play together.

G – Guide them to a solution. "Wow. It seems like you have come up with a lot of options. You should be proud of yourselves! Which one would work for both of you?"

If your kids were play fighting with foam noodles and now it's turning aggressive

A – Walk to them, separate them if necessary and safe for you to do so. Say, "It seems like this game has gotten a little aggressive. Do you need help sorting it out?"

L – If they say yes, listen to both sides.

Child 1: We were playing but then she hit me in the face. We said no faces!

Child 2: It was an accident. These noodles are long. I didn't mean to.

O - Offer your understanding of the situation. "It seems like [Child 1] is upset because [Child 2] hit them in the face and [Child 2] is frustrated because she didn't mean to. Is that right?"

N - Name some ideas.

You: What can we do to resolve this?

Child 1&2: [silence]

You: Do you think you'd like to apologize for hurting [Child 1]?

Child 2: Yeah. I guess. I'm sorry. I should have been more careful with my noodle.

Child 1: Maybe we should have a rule that we only hit below the shoulders.

Child 2: Or we could play something else?

Child 1: Maybe we could knock down some stuffed animals with the pool noodles?

G – Guide them to choose. "I think I see where this is going, but it seems like you have really come up with some good ideas. Do you need any help choosing the best one for the both of you?"

Chapter 6

Oops! They Did it Again.

Teaching Your Kids to Apologize

The Basics:

O - Own up: say what you did without qualifying

O - Other person's feelings: state them

P - Plan for the future: explain it

S - Sorry: say it

The Thought Process:

I'm an avid reality TV watcher. To be more specific, I love any of the Real Housewives series. And one of my very favorite things to see on one of those shows is how very horrible grown adult women can be at apologizing. The mind truly boggles.

They will classically say something along the lines of "I'm sorry that *you felt* xyz," or "I'm sorry, *but* blah blah blah," or "I apologize. I didn't mean to do yada yada yada." If you've ever been on the receiving end of one of those kinds of apologies, you've probably left the conversation just as upset as when you entered it. Even if the other person did actually feel remorse, you wouldn't know it from those lines. And you'd probably doubt any real change in behavior would occur.

In their defense, most of the Real Housewives were born in the 1900s; and as such, were never taught how to apologize by their parents, teachers, or other responsible adults. We don't know what we don't know. This is just coming to me right now, but maybe Bravo TV should hire me to teach these women what to do. Nah. That would ruin some very good television. But I'll still help you with your kids if that's okay with you.

Ideally, you'd teach these steps to your kids prior to any offense, but sometimes you'll have to do it in the moment. Of course, a wonderful way to do this is to model apologizing yourself.

Imagine if you made a parenting snafu and then APOLOGIZED to your KIDS. They would learn so much from that gesture - how to do it, why you should, how it feels to get a good apology, and that their parent respects them enough to do so.

You could also do an apology practice session after you notice they are lacking in this department (because of course they are). After you've apologized for something, you could say, "Did you feel better after I apologized? Apologies are tough but so helpful. There is an easy way to remember how to do it. Can I teach you?"

How it Works:

O - Own up to what you did. Simply say out loud the thing that you did. Accept responsibility.

O - Other person's feelings. Try to guess how you made them feel. It's okay to be wrong. They will tell you if you are.

P – Plan for the future. Tell them your plans to fix this and/or not do it again.

S – Say "I'm sorry." Those words can be so difficult but so powerful.

Some Sample Scripts:

If you lost your cool with your kids

O – "I yelled at you instead of taking a moment to calm myself down."

O – "You probably felt scared when I shouted."

P – "In the future, I will do my best to take some deep breaths when I am frustrated."

S – "I'm so sorry."

If your child breaks your lamp, they could say

O – "I broke the green lamp this morning."

O – "I know you've had that for a long time, so you're probably upset."

P – "I'm going to do some extra chores to earn money to buy you a new lamp. I noticed the garage is getting messy. Can I help to clean it out?"

S – "I'm really sorry."

Chapter 7

STOP!

Stopping Kids From Hitting (And Other Aggressive Behaviors)

The Basics:

S - Separate for safety

T - Take time to calm down & find out what happened

O - Offer better choices

P - Practice

The Thought Process:

Have you ever, as an adult, honked your horn excessively at another driver or banged on the table after stubbing your toe? Maybe not. Maybe you have developed healthier habits for calming yourself down when adrenaline is high. I'm willing to bet you have done something at least mildly destructive in a moment of pain or fear.

For our children, especially toddlers and preschoolers who haven't had time to build up a calm-down toolbox, physical aggression is a natural response to explosive feelings. Until they have had lots of opportunities to practice, the easiest way for them to express their anger is to hit, kick, or grab things. Unfortunately, these behaviors can be dangerous for their siblings or other children around them, and as parents we have a duty to stop them from hurting others.

How it Works:

When you notice conversations are getting heated with your young kids, it would be best to step in before physical violence occurs. Prevention is much more helpful than reactivity. If it's already reached that point- if one child has hit or kicked another, swoop in and *stop* it.

S - Separate for safety. Physically separate children if possible. You can pick one up, put something between them, or just use words to tell them to move. Afterwards, if one child (or an adult) was definitely the one being threatened, ask them if they feel safe. See if they would like to go somewhere else while you talk to the aggressor.

T - Take time to calm down and find out what happened. If things have gotten violent, there are a few ways it could go. The offending child may feel immediately guilty and start crying. They might feel the pressure was released and be surprisingly calm. They might still be angry and have lots of adrenaline coursing through their veins. It's helpful if you've practiced deep breaths, hugs, closing eyes and repeating a mantra or another calm down technique to bring the energy down first. And then ask them what happened. Try to really listen and empathize.

O – Offer better choices. You can either supply these yourself or ask your child to help you brainstorm some ideas for what they could do next time.

P – Practice. This might feel funny at first, but if you can actually take a moment to role play either right then or another calm moment, it's more likely your child will remember what to do next time they feel frustrated.

Some Sample Scripts:

Your 4 year-old knocks down your 3 year-old's tower, and 3 hits 4.

S - Walk into the room and separate kids physically so both are safe. Say to 4: "Are you okay? Would you like to stay here while I talk to 3 or would you like to play over there?"

T - Say to 3: "You got upset and hit 4. What happened?" Allow 3 to explain what happened. If 3 is reluctant or unable to tell you what happened, you can guess. "Did 4 knock over your tower? Did it make you mad?"

O - You: "It can be really frustrating when someone knocks over something you've been working on. Next time, tell 4 'I've been working hard on that. Please keep your hands to yourself.' If 4 still knocks over your tower, what can you do to keep calm?"

3: "Deep breaths, walk away, or tell 4 I am mad."

You: "Those are some great ideas. Which one do you think would work best for you?"

P - You: "Let's practice the one you picked. Do you want to pretend to be you first or 4 first?"

You tell your child it's time to clean up the playroom and they throw a toy at you.

S – Move your body away from your child. Say "I won't let you hurt me. I'll move over here to stay safe."

T – Say "You threw a toy at me. It seems like you weren't ready to stop playing. It's hard to stop when you are having fun, but it's not okay to throw things. Is that what happened?" Allow your child to respond until you understand.

O – Say "Next time, you can ask me for 2 more minutes or you can ask if you can clean up after dinner. If you are frustrated you could go to your calm down corner or do something else that helps you. What do you think would work for you?" Allow your child to brainstorm ideas as well.

P – Later in the day or the next day; when everything is calm. "Let's practice what you'll do next time. First, you pretend to be me, and I'll show you what I would do. Then, you can practice."

Chapter 8

ALTS

Alternatives (or Choices)

The Basics:

A - Assistance

L - Location

T - Time

S - Same but different

The Thought Process:

All day long, whether we want to or not, we spend a lot of time telling our kids what to do. How many of these requests have you made before 9 am on a single day?

Time to wake up.

Come have breakfast.

Go brush your teeth.

Get dressed for school.

Grab your backpack.

Buckle your seatbelt.

Even though we aren't intending to be bossy with those commands- we are just trying to keep our kids alive, healthy, and organized- they will likely feel as though we are controlling them. There aren't too many choices kids get to make in a day. The more we can empower them to make their own choices, the better they will feel. And if they are feeling in control of some decisions, they will likely have less opposition to your requests.

You've probably heard before that offering kids choices can help to alleviate power struggles, but many times in the moment it can be difficult to come up with two options. And more importantly, it can be tough to come up with two options that are acceptable to both parties. Your choices; for example, should not be, "Do your homework OR you're grounded." Only one of those choices is reasonable for your child. The child doesn't truly have a choice in that situation.

It also isn't as helpful for younger children to just let them pick any old thing. If your friend asked you, "Where do you want to eat?" you'd have a much harder time answering than if they said, "Sushi, tacos, or pizza?" The same goes for our kids.

And a little ending thought: whenever you are finished giving your options, you could say something like, "it's up to you," or "your choice" to really boost the idea that it is your child's decision. It's a little cherry on top.

How it Works:

To make sure you have plenty of choices at the ready, there are some options that can be molded to fit pretty much any situation. Remember these "ALTS" or alternatives:

A - Assistance: Do they want your help or can they do it by themselves?

L - Location: Where would they like to do this?

T - Time: When would they like to do this?

S - Same but different. Are there 2 things that are very similar that you could offer?

Samples:

Assistance

"Can you put on your boots by yourself or would you like some help?"

"Let me know if you can reach the faucet yourself or if you need my help washing your hands."

Location

"Do you want to brush your teeth in your bathroom or mine?"

"Do you want to put your shoes on in the house or the car?"

Time

"Would you like to clean the playroom now or after dinner?"

"I need to talk to you for 10 minutes. Would during breakfast or after school be better for you?"

Same but different

"Would you rather wear the blue shirt or the red shirt?"

"We're eating pasta for dinner. If you don't want that, you can have a sandwich or yogurt and fruit. You pick."

A Bonus Way to Remember The ALTS:

To the tune of "Twinkle Twinkle Little Star"

Now or later? Here or there?

Either time or anywhere.

This or that? Which one will win? (Even though they're the same thing).

Would you like a little help or can you do it by yourself?

Chapter 9

DO IT!

When You Have to Get Your Kids Ready, Like Now

The Basics:

D - Daily Schedule

O - One Direction

I - Independence

T - Time

! - Excitement or Fun

The Thought Process:

Sure, we want to validate our children's emotions as often as possible, but there are days when we just need to get out the door. Doctor's appointments, playdates, school events- whatever the situation- there are ways to encourage participation and compliance without you screaming and pulling out your hair. (More on emotional regulation is coming; for both you and your kids. I promise.)

Try to remember also that kids don't care about our schedules. They don't feel the pressure that we feel to be on time, but they do feel the stress that you exhibit in those moments. If you work outside the home, think about a time your boss was stressed and the entire office felt like they were walking on egg shells. No one wants to be in that environment, so prepare as much as you can ahead of time to prevent time crunches. If you need to, set an easy-to-grab breakfast on the counter or put your kids to sleep in their clothes; whatever you need to do the night before, you won't miss those extra minutes of sleep before you go to sleep as much as you'll miss the ability to snooze in the morning. Or maybe that's just me.

How it Works:

Daily Schedule - sit down with your child(ren) the night before or earlier in the week and go over what the day will look like. If they have an idea of what's going to happen it's less likely they will be anxious and do things to prevent getting in the car. Bonus points if you can plan something fun after a less desirable activity. "We're going to the park after the doctor," etc.

One direction at a time: Make your directions short, clear, and positive. Give them one task at a time; and when they finish, give them another. If you don't have time to tell them what to do a step at a time, you could give them a written or visual to do list. It depends on your child's ability as well. What will they be able to handle?

Independence: Give your child a sense of independence by offering as many choices as you can. If you can think of them ahead of time, that would be helpful in the moment. Go back to the ALTS chapter if you need help coming up with choices.

Time: Just like you don't like stopping what you're doing immediately when someone wants your attention, your child will likely be frustrated if you expect them to stop in the middle of an activity. You can either give them options for time or set a timer so they know they have to find a stopping point.

! Fun or Excitement: Try to turn the boring task of leaving the house into a game if you can. I've added a list that have worked for us at the end of the chapter. If you can't do that, using a silly voice might even help out. Kids love novelty and playing. You knew that, though.

Samples:

D: Go over the activities for a busy day:

    -verbally, and/or with a written or pictorial list

    -the night before, the morning of, or earlier in the week

    -and show your child the preferred activities that are sprinkled in

O: Give short, clear directions like this:

    -brush your teeth

    -find your shoes

    -pick one stuffy to bring

I: Give your child(ren) choices like this:

    -You can put on your shoes before we leave or you can put them on when we get there. Which do you prefer?

    -Would you like a yogurt squeeze or apple sauce pouch for the car?

    -After the dentist, should we go to the park or the library?

T: Let your child finish what they are doing or set a timer to let them know when you are leaving.

!: Make leaving fun or exciting! Play a game if you can. Pretend to be:

- Spies on a mission
- Astronauts preparing to take off
- Race car drivers
- Movie stars dodging paparazzi
- Campers leaving for a trip
- Soldiers following orders
- Cheerleaders learning a routine

Chapter 10

WHY Are They Doing That Thing, AGAIN?

Addressing the Cause to Find a Solution

The Basics:

W - What are they doing?

H - How is that meeting a need of theirs?

Y - You there: What can YOU do to Teach, Help, Explain, Redirect, or Excuse them?

The Thought Process:

It's funny we've gotten to chapter 10 without using this acronym, because "why?" has got to be the most commonly used word in most homes- at least those with small children. Kids are always asking why they have to do things, why things are the way they are, and just plain "why?" (usually as a way to drive us bananas, I think).

And parents are always wondering *why* our kids are doing whatever it is they are doing. Some of their choices seem so ridiculous, that we can't begin to comprehend why they would; in fact, choose to do those things. Here's the thing, though. If you ask a child "Why did you do that?" Most of the time, they have no clue. Many times, there are no reasons (or at least ones that they recognize) behind their actions. They are merely acting on impulse; as if a button was pushed and they are simply robots designed to obey the commands of their whims.

If we want to stop a certain problematic behavior from continuing to happen, it often falls to us, the parents, to figure out the why. If we can, we are more likely to be able to help our kids achieve their goals in a more meaningful or appropriate way. It's important to address the underlying communication behind our kids' actions rather than the behavior itself, because many different needs could result in the same behavior. If we just eliminate the behavior by punishing the child, the need will go unmet. If the need goes unmet, the behavior is likely to recur.

A note before we talk about understanding our kids' needs: sometimes there are unrelated issues that may be causing your child to act in a way that is undesirable. For example, many kids spend all day at school holding it together and they let loose at home (because they know you love them no matter what). Sometimes your child will act bossy or aggressive towards you, siblings, or pets, because they have spent all day being told what to do by parents, other kids, and teachers. They need a chance to feel empowered. It can be difficult to figure out what the related cause is, so give yourself time and grace. Some ideas that might help: Try to put yourself in their position. Imagine what their days are like. Notice what happens *immediately* before specific behaviors.

How it Works:

W: What is your child doing? First, identify the behavioral concern: are they being aggressive, whining, jumping on furniture, biting, wiping boogers on their sleeve, throwing tissues on the floor, etc.? Try to help your child with one specific measurable behavior at a time. You could even track it, keep a tally sheet, and tell your child, "I noticed that 10 times this week, you threw your laundry on the ground instead of in the hamper." Notice the behavior in a very specific way.

H: How is that meeting a need? Depending on the age of your child and the sensitivity of the issue, you can either work with them to determine the need or you can attempt to figure it out on your own. You can always check in with them to see if you are correct. If the need in this example was *I need it to be a little easier to put my laundry in the hamper,* you could say, "It seems like the hamper is in an inconvenient place for you. Is that what's making it difficult for you to get the laundry in the right place?"

Y: You (there)- How can YOU help them?

You could:

- *Teach* them a new and/or better way to do it : "Why don't we move the hamper to the bathroom? Would that help?"
- *Help* them to do it in the moment: "Before bath-time, let's walk to the hamper together and put the clothes in this week."
- *Explain* why the way they are doing it is causing a problem: "Bud, when you leave your clothes on the floor, the dog might chew them up or they might start to stink."

- *Redirect* them to do something else: "Okay. I get it. You hate cleaning, but you LOVE basketball. Why don't we see if we can score 10 points by earning 2 points per piece of clothes?"
- *Excuse* their behavior and let it go (in rare cases): "Seems like you're having a really tough week and maybe laundry just isn't the most important thing. I get it. Want to talk about anything?"

Samples:

Although there is already a sample above, I wanted to share an example of why it's important to think about the underlying reasons for a behavior. If you think about biting, each of these needs requires a different solution.

WHAT are they doing?	HOW does it meet a need?	YOU- what can YOU do?
Biting parents/siblings	They are bored. It keeps their mouth busy.	Give them something else stimulating for their brain or mouth.
Biting parents/siblings	They are lonely. They want your attention.	Give them attention ahead of time. Let them do an activity near you.
Biting parents/siblings	Their teeth hurt. They are teething.	Try different teething relief techniques: teethers, something cold, something sour.
Biting parents/siblings	They are frustrated. They are unable to accomplish something.	Help them with whatever they are doing.
Biting parents/siblings	They are angry. They don't like what someone did.	Teach them other ways to emotionally regulate: deep breaths, calm down cream, hugging a stuffy, etc.

Chapter 11

THE ABCs

Helping Your Kids Clean Their Rooms

The Basics:

T - Trash

H - Hamper

E - Everywhere Else

A - Away

B - Bed

Cs - Clean Surfaces

The Thought Process:

    Hey. Let's go run a marathon tomorrow. Better yet, let's write a book together. Wait. I've got it. Let's host a party for 200 people. If your anxiety is at a level 3,000 at the mention of any of these events, I am with you. The reason most people don't do any of those tasks (at least daily) is because they are overwhelming, huge, daunting proposals. Even if you told me I had to run a marathon six months from now, I wouldn't know where to start.

And that's how our kids; our brand-new-to-this-world babies, feel when we say, "Go clean your room!" If your kids are anything like my child (or like me, tbh) there a little doom piles everywhere; collections of mismatched bric-a-brac waiting to be deposited in their rightful places. When the sunlight shines through a window in their room; if they're anything like me, dust and hair will dance in the beams. And if I wrote in my planner, "Clean the house," for tomorrow, I would be frozen staring at the page for an hour before my brain could get itself together to start the task. Again, I'm guessing I'm a little bit like your child on this one.

Now, if I write down that Monday and Thursday are for tidying, Tuesday is for dusting, Wednesday is for vacuuming, and the weekends are for laundry; I might have more success. Having one short, concrete task at a time is much easier than a broad, overarching idea of a task. If you break things down, and order them, it's easier than THE ABCs.

How it Works:

Before we get into the nitty gritty, I want to encourage you to do a tiny thought experiment. If your child's bedroom is not up to your standards, what does that mean to you? Of course, if they have plates of food or anything unsafe lying around, that's not great. But what does it really mean if their room is a little messy? Yes. We want to teach our kids cleaning skills, but the truth is, to them cleaning is probably just not that important. (Neither is being on time, but that's a different topic.) You constantly telling them to keep their personal space; which probably doesn't actually affect you that much, clean will probably cause more stress on your relationship than the good the cleanliness would cause. Maybe this is something we can teach our kids while also managing our own expectations.

But anyway, here we go…

T - Trash

H - Hamper

E - Everywhere Else

A - Away

B - Bed

Cs - Clean Surfaces

Make a poster for or with your kids with these (or your own chosen) steps on it. If you make it together, talk about it as you are creating it. Find out what they already know about cleaning their room and add your opinions. After you are done, hang or store it in their room somewhere that they can access it whenever they need it. You might hang it inside the closet or put it in their sock drawer. It doesn't need to be visible all the time.

The first few times, you will probably need to stay in the room with them and support them through the cleaning process. After that, you could remind them of the steps before hand and then check in at different intervals. And eventually, they will know how to do it by themselves.

Samples:

T - Trash: First, they will go around their room and collect and dispose of any trash or recycling that they see.

H - Hamper: Next, it's Hamper Time™. Your child will put any dirty laundry in the hamper. If it's something they plan to wear again before washing; like jeans, they can put them in a designated location.

E – Everywhere Else: If you can get your child a bin from the Dollar Tree, that would be super helpful here. For this step, they collect everything that has been taken into their room but actually belongs in a different room. They then distribute those items back to their rightful places.

A – Away: Put everything away; where it belongs. Labeled bins are your friend here. You can label with pictures or words so that kids can see exactly where to put things. Don't want to buy a bunch of bins? I get it. I used to reject the bin life too. If you have another system for organizing things on shelves or in drawers, great!

B – Bed: Make the bed. Back in 2014, Jolie Kerr, the author of *My Boyfriend Barfed in my Handbag…And Other Things You Can't Ask Martha* challenged me (and her very engaged podcast audience) to spend the month of March making our beds every day in an activity she called LAMOB: Let's All Make Our Beds. I was never a bed-maker before, but she argued that it could take as little as 90 seconds. I had to challenge that. But she was right. I just had to pull up the covers and straighten the pillows. It makes the whole room seem neater and makes for a more comfy night's sleep later on. Ever since that challenge, I have been a bed-maker. I think if you show your kids a 90 second bed making routine, they will be too.

Cs - Clean Surfaces: This one will depend on what furniture you have in your home, but this is the actual dirt-removal step of the process. Start at the top of the room so that any dislodged dirt/dust/gresidue™ (that's greasy residue) will fall to the floor- the last cleanable surface. Do you want your child to clean fan blades? Up to you. Do you want your child to wipe mirrors? Up to you. Do you want your child to vacuum? Also, up to you. Just make sure you tell them ahead of time and practice with them before releasing them into the wild.

Chapter 12

TRAUMA

How We Can Support Our Kids Through Tough Times

The Basics:

T - Touch

R - Routines

A - Acknowledge their feelings

U - Use calm down strategies

M - Maintain composure

A - Answer questions (so they don't make up what happened in their head)

The Thought Process:

It's hard to think about, but our kids will all go through some form of trauma in their lives. Some events are more difficult or delicate than others, but all require processing. Your child may lose a grandparent, a parent, or a pet. There may be a fire, a flood, or another natural disaster. They may witness their parent or sibling being abused, getting into an accident, or getting sick. The list is endless. And it's important that we address these issues as soon as possible to prevent deeper levels of damage. If necessary, involving a school counselor or family therapist would be helpful as well.

One easy way to determine if your child has been traumatized by a recent event is if they are repeating the story, acting out the events physically, or having recurring dreams about the events. It's almost as if the event is stuck in their brain and they are "chewing it up" in a way so it can be digested. If you notice one of these patterns, or if you assume something that happened to your child may have been traumatic, you can use these strategies to help them process it.

How it Works:

Touch: Reinforce your bond with your child through physical touch IF; and this is very important, the touch isn't triggering with regard to the event or any other trauma. If your child recoils, pulls away, or asks you to stop; pay attention. Otherwise, a hand on the shoulder, a hug, or a hand squeeze can be reassuring.

Routine: Try to keep routines as close to normal as possible. Of course, there will likely be some shake-ups, but humans feel safe in our routines. I went back to work 3 days after my mom passed away because sitting at home and thinking about it all day was too much for me. Having things to do gave me a sense of comfort. Seeing familiar faces gave me calm.

Acknowledge their feelings: Even if it feels like a silly thing to you, if your child has been deeply impacted by an event, recognize and acknowledge those feelings. It's okay for them to feel however they do after something happens. It's our job to teach them to work through those feelings so they don't linger in them forever.

Use Calm Down Strategies: Use them yourself and narrate what you're doing so that your child can be reminded of them without you stopping to reteach in the moment.

Maintain Composure: If something happened to the whole family, it is not your child's job to comfort you or stay strong for the family. To be honest, it's not really yours either. If you experience a traumatic event as a family, it's okay to let your child see you feel emotions about it. But there does come a time where as a parent you'll need to keep it together for your kids. If you spend 6 months in your room crying, your child will have suffered the same initial loss as you but then have suffered a long-term loss of parental attachment and attention as well.

Answer questions appropriately: If you've ever gotten the "we need to talk" text, you know how the mind works with limited information. You will start to guess, fill in gaps, and think of the worst-case scenario. Tell your kids age-appropriate amounts of information so they don't make up something worse in their heads.

Sample:

Your child's dog is hit by a car

T: Offer your child a hug and allow them to cry as much as they need to

R: Talk to your child about possibly missing one day of school to be sad but then returning the following day. You can respect the grieving process but not let it take over.

A: Say, "Fluffy was the best dog. He always snuggled you when you were sad. You probably wish you could snuggle him now to help you feel better. That's so hard. This is really sad." And give them space to share their feelings.

U: Say, "I'm feeling really sad. I'm going to take a bubble bath, put on my comfiest pajamas, and then snuggle on the sofa with a blanket. Do you want to join me?"

M: It's okay for you to cry too. Try to let your child's emotions be at the center though.

A: Answer questions as honestly as you can without giving too much detail.

    Did it hurt? Probably not. It was quick.

    Where is he? He's in our hearts. We can see him in our dreams.

    Will he ever come back? No, sweetheart. He won't come back.

Chapter 13

4Hs: Be There for Them

How to be there for your kids when they are upset

The Basics:

Hear them

Hug them

Help them

Humor them

The Thought Process:

You've witnessed your child go through something traumatic or they have just told you about something that happened to them. You've already said, "Ugh. I'm so sorry. That sucks. Thank you for telling me." And now you're ready to empathize your little butt off. But how?

If we've done our jobs right, and our kids come to us with their problems, we should feel so proud of ourselves. If it happens for me, I know I will be grateful that I'm the one to give my son support and advice if he wants it. It's so hard to know what people need in tough situations, and if we make the wrong move, we can worry that we will scare our kids from ever telling us anything again.

I HIGHLY RECOMMEND every parent read The Rabbit Listened by Cory Doerrfeld. It's a kids' book, but it gives such a relatable perspective on how all the different responses to trauma might affect the victim. To summarize though, when something bad happened to the main character, Taylor, many of his animal friends came to see him. Most of the animals wanted to talk to him, to fix the problem, or start over again. There was one animal, the rabbit, who just sat there with him and listened. And that was what Taylor really needed. If you want to "be there" for your child, here's what you can do.

How it Works:

Hear them: Tell them that you appreciate that they confided in you. You could ask if they want to talk more about it. You could also just sit there and wait. A lot of times people will start talking when there is empty space to fill. And one other option is to tell them that you will be there whenever they are ready to talk. Maybe now they need time to mentally process.

Hug them: This is pretty self-explanatory. Many times, in a difficult situation a hug will help to reduce our anxiety and sadness. Your child will mirror your breathing patterns and their hearts will start to beat at the same pace as yours. The same effect can be felt when you simply hold your child's hand or rub their back. A gentle touch, when desired, can work wonders. Of course, if your child scoots away, arches their body, or recoils at your touch; don't try to force it. And although it may be hurtful, try not to take offense.

Help them: Many times, going further than hearing your child is unnecessary, but if they seem open to your guidance, this would be an okay time to offer it. You could start this conversation by saying, "I'd like to offer some suggestions/tell you a similar story that happened to me. Are you open to that or do you want to deal with it on your own?" Or "Do you want advice or comfort?"

You could share a similar story to what they are going through. You could ask them to name solutions and help them to see where each idea might lead. You could offer your suggestions as well.

When offering help, try to anticipate what they might need and your abilities and offer the intersection of those two things specifically. When someone is grieving, upset, hurt, or stressed; it can be overwhelming to think of what they need for help. They may know they need assistance, but not know what they need or what you are actually willing to do. Giving them 2-3 ideas can narrow it down for them.

Humor them: This isn't the traditional use of the word "humor them," but I was limited in H words here. You know your child better than anyone. If they are in a space to tolerate it, you could remind them of a funny experience or crack a joke. Sometimes it's too soon, but if it's appropriate, laughter is the best medicine.

Samples:

Hear them: Your dog ran away and you haven't been able to find him for 2 days? You must be so worried and sad. I'm so sorry. Tell me more about what's been going on since he went missing. How are you feeling? What have you been doing to get through it.

OR

Your dog ran away. I can't imagine how worried you are. Do you want to talk about it? I'll be here when you're ready.

Hug them: No one wanted to play with you at recess because they thought your shoes were stupid? And you sat by yourself the whole time? That sounds so rough. Ugh. People can be so mean. Do you want a hug? Can I sit near you?

Help them: Your science fair project got destroyed by a raccoon? Oh no! You've been working so hard on that for the last 4 weeks. I'm so sorry. Can I write an email to your teacher for you or help you try to put it back together?

OR

Oh my goodness. I can't believe your friend kissed your boyfriend. That sounds so disrespectful and hurtful and I really appreciate you trusting me with that. I have a similar story that happened to me. Do you think hearing it would help?

Humor them: I can't believe you broke your foot walking down the stairs at school. That's such a bummer that you have to wear a cast to prom. Hey, do you think they offer a discount on only one shoe? Maybe you can finally afford some Louboutins.

Chapter 14

HOTT

Trying to Figure Out Why Our Kids Are Frustrated (or Hott)

The Basics:

H - Hungry

O - Over-stimulated

T - Tired (or sick)

T - Triggered

The Thought Process:

It doesn't matter if you're two, four, seven, sixteen, or forty-two; it is still possible for you to have a tantrum or meltdown. The reasons may be different. The way you express it may be different. The intensity may be different. But we all have bad days and we all have a breaking point.

Remember a tantrum is different from a meltdown. A tantrum occurs when a person doesn't get their way. They are still able to talk; and to some extent, reason. A meltdown occurs when a person has lost control of their emotions due to overwhelm. They may be in fight or flight mode. They will be unable to process what you are saying or respond appropriately.

Both of these situations are more likely to happen if your child is hungry, over-stimulated, tired (or sick), or triggered. It can help to pretend you are playing the Sims and monitoring all of your child's levels during the day. If their levels are off, it's possible you'll be in for some tricky interactions. And a little forethought and noticing can go a long way to making sure you get to keep playing the game without your child's Sim character getting taken away by Child Protective Services. (Did you know that happens when you don't meet their needs in the game? I just learned that.) (*The Sims Wiki*, 2023).

How it Works:

Hungry- This one is fairly obvious. Kids have two stomachs: the meal stomach and the snack stomach and both must be filled constantly. Okay, I'm goofin'. They have the one stomach that all humans have, but it *does* seem like theirs behave in a different way from ours. There are days where they will eat more food than an adult female grizzly bear, and some days where they will eat a single Cheerio. We rarely get any warning as to which sort of day it will be. It's best to be prepared for either situation. Ask your child at multiple times during the day if they would like a snack. Have a snack area set up in your pantry where they can grab options if you are not available to regularly provide them. And this is crucial, never leave home without snacks. You know this already. All parents must have one packet of fruit snacks and one squished granola bar in their possession at all times. And so it is written.

Over-Stimulated- Try to think about your child's day before it happens and as it is progressing. Especially if they are neurodivergent; too many lights, sounds, smells, and people can physically wear them down, but these things can affect all children. If you know your child can get easily overstimulated, bring comfort items like stuffies, noise-canceling headphones, and even a tablet so they can "zone out" for a little while with a familiar show or game. I know there are lots of conflicting feelings about tablets and screen time; but even as an adult, after a long day I need a little TV time to wind down. Try to pay attention to your child's reactions to certain lighting situations, smells, and sounds. If they cover their ears, recoil, do some sort of stimming behavior like flapping their arms or repeating a sound; take it seriously. They may be physically uncomfortable. Try to take them to an area with as little stimulation as possible. A dark(ish), quiet, small room is a nice place for most people to re-center.

Tired/Sick- Getting into a regular sleep schedule is a challenge for parents of kids of all ages. As our kids grow up, they need different amounts of sleep and will tend to sleep at different times of the day. It's tough to stay on top of the changes let alone help them to manage their schedules. If you can, try to help your child get enough sleep every day. It will make a huge impact on their abilities to regulate their emotions.

When kids get sick, their abilities to stay calm are lowered as well. And what's especially tricky is that sometimes they can't explain it to you. My son doesn't even know he is sick most of the time. I'll ask if he has a sore throat and he says, "Oh yeah. I think my mouth hurts." Kids aren't always able to tell you exactly what's going on in their bodies so if you suspect they are ill, take their temperature or do a body check-in.

Triggered- Has something specific set off the behavior? What happened right before your child hit their brother? Were you on your phone? Did they want the toy? What was the thing that happened immediately before?

Alternatively, has something been going on recently that has caused them to be triggered? A loss, trauma, or serious event could send ripples of behavioral issues. Big changes can cause problems too. Have you moved, started a new school/job, is there a new baby, is there a new spouse? Anything like that is something that can cause your child to be "set-off" more easily. Teaching your child calm down strategies ahead of time, when they are calm, is beneficial to addressing the problems before they start.

Chapter 15

WHOA

How to Respond to Shocking Statements from your child

The Basics

W - Wait to respond

H - Help name feelings

O - Offer a replacement phrase

A - Ask questions

The Thought Process

    When your sweet, innocent baby starts to talk it will be a series of Kid Rock lyrics: ba widaba da bang da bang diggy diggy, etc. Eventually, they will be able to string together a few words like: cookie mama NOW. And then, they will more than likely reach a point where they say some pretty clever things like: being handsome is all about being yourself. AND THEN, they will get to a ridiculous stage where they say things that you thought were reserved for Stephen King novels: Mama, I want to kick your head off and watch blood come out of your neck.

Yes, your baby will say stuff like that, and then they will probably laugh. I know. I don't like it either, but it's a very normal stage in your child's development. As with a lot of things, they are testing boundaries and looking to see what kind of response you give them. So, your response here is pretty important.

How it Works

When your precious bundle of joy says something that makes you want to sleep with one eye open, remember WHOA.

W – Wait to respond until you've had a chance to process. It can be tempting to jump in right away and say something like, "We don't say 'eyeball stab' in this house," but if you can take a second to regulate your emotions before responding, you'll be more effective.

H – Help them name what they are actually feeling. You could say, "You're mad at Mommy because I didn't make you macaroni with hot dogs in it" or "You're disappointed because you wanted the green cup" or "You're feeling silly because you are full of Halloween candy."

O – Offer a replacement phrase.

When you're mad at me, you can say, "I'm mad at you, Mommy."

When things don't go your way, you can say, "I'm so frustrated."

When you're upset about something, you can say, "I'm so sad or disappointed."

When you're in a goofy mood, you could ask me if I want to be silly with you.

A - Ask questions to find out more.

    Where did you hear/see that?

    What do you mean when you say that?

    How do you think that makes me feel?

    How do you feel when you say those things?

    Do you need a hug or some attention?

    Can I help you with what you're going through?

PART III

Other Helpful Stuff

Chapter 16

The Nurse and the Narrator

When You Have More Than One Child

Pretty frequently on social media, I'll get comments like this: Just out of curiosity, do you have more than one child? Or: this would never work with all three of my kids melting down together at once. I get it. A lot of my advice, and respectful parenting advice in general is geared to situations where you are able to give many minutes of undivided attention to one child. For many parents, this is not your reality, and it can be tempting to just throw in the towel (or throw a towel at parenting content creators who just don't get you).

Before you take it to that level with me, I will level with you. I only have one child. So, yes. My parenting journey is probably considerably easier than a lot of yours. Granted, we have our challenges. I won't get into them here. But as the Notorious B.I.G. said, "More kids more problems," or something like that*. I was; however, an elementary school teacher for 11 years. I had new kids and new challenges presented to me every school year; new personalities to learn and new conflicts to manage. For 5 of those years, I was an art teacher, so I had a class and a half in my room all day. Imagine 35 kindergarteners with scissors and glue and sharing and emotions. So I may not fully get it, but I get it.

*he did not say that

Since I don't fully get your individual situation, I can't prescribe a specific solution for it. I can give you an idea that will help when you have multiple volcanoes to address at once. I call it The Nurse and the Narrator. First, you will pretend to be a nurse and then a narrator. Makes sense, right?

In your nurse role, you will perform triage duties. If you don't know what triage is, it's the procedure by which emergency room nurses determine who needs treatment first. So, in a New Year's Eve at the ER type situation, you'll first check to see if anyone is physically hurt. That would require immediate attention. As a good nurse would, inform the other "patients" that you will be with them shortly. You'll just need to apply bandages to the wounds of the injured.

Then, assess whether or not the remaining patients can stay in the same room as each other or if they'll need to be put into individual recovery rooms (i.e., the tension is too high or one child is noticeably more upset). Again, keep them informed. "Your sister is screaming and needs me right now. I'm going to try to help her calm down. Would you like to sit in the hallway or go to your bedroom?" If they can stay in the same room, you can move to narrator phase.

As the narrator, you have two goals: buy yourself some time while you try to figure out what to do and understand the problem more fully. Just start narrating what you see. (If you're wrong, this is when your kids will likely pipe up and tell you).

"Brother, it seems like you built a fort out of couch cushions and when Sister jumped onto it, it collapsed. She bonked her knee…"

"IT WAS MY HIP!"

"Okay, I think I'm understanding better now. Sister bonked her hip on the floor and it hurt. Brother, you're feeling disappointed because your fort is destroyed and you'll have to start from scratch."

"YEAH AND I TOLD HER NOT TO COME IN HERE!"

Just a few sentences and a few seconds and now you can start to formulate a solution or empower them to do it on their own.

You may re-do the triage at this point to see if they need to be separated and cool down. At least though, you can now take some time to problem solve; hopefully as a team.

Chapter 17

Emotional Regulation

The Steps, The Signs, The Strategies

Emotional regulation is a fancy way of saying, "the ability to stay relatively calm or respond appropriately despite what triggers and obstacles are thrown at you." Some people are naturally better at this than others. Children and neurodivergent people struggle with emotional regulation until they are taught strategies to deal with big emotions and given many chances to practice using them. Many adults have difficulty staying emotionally regulated because nobody taught them effective ways to self-soothe. Someone who is emotionally *dys*regulated might be described as explosive, unhinged, or aggressive.

Teaching your child (and yourself) to be better regulated does not mean that you will stop feeling unpleasant emotions.

Rather, it will lessen the chances that they will get stuck in a meltdown or tantrum for an extended period of time. It may be necessary for them to process the feelings later even if they have used one or more of the emotional regulation strategies.

For example, let's say your child wants a balloon from the grocery store, but you look at the price tag and see that for some reason a balloon now costs $17.99 (I wish I was making this up). Your child may get very disappointed when you tell them the balloon is not on the list. They may start to cry or shout at you. While disappointment is a reasonable emotion, shouting in the grocery store is a behavior that you would probably like your child to limit. Crying, if done to self-soothe for a few minutes, is not a problem; but when a child is crying about a balloon for 30 minutes while you are trying to pick up the weekly groceries, that is not ideal. If you have taught your child some of the self-regulation strategies on this chart, you could remind them or model them in the moment. When you get home from the store, you could talk to your child about what happened. "You seemed to really want that balloon. What a bummer it cost so much. It's okay to feel sad about it."

All feelings are okay, but if we allow feelings of upset to linger for too long, they can cause damage to our bodies and brains. That's why it's helpful to have some regulation skills in your emotional first aid kit to pull out during emergencies. Then, once you've addressed the initial exterior wound, you can see if there's deeper damage later when you have more time or assistance.

The Steps:

You can remember a simplified way to teach emotional regulation to your kids with this song to the tune of *Head, Shoulders, Knees, and Toes.*

Your brain and body give you clues (give you clues)

You have big feelings I do too (I do too)

I'll show you what I do to make it through (make it through)

And prove that I'll be here for you (here for you)

1. *Your brain and body give you clues:* teach your child how to look for clues that their brain and/or body give them that they are about to have a big emotions. Start by pointing out facial expressions and body movements other people, book characters, actors, and family members are displaying: *His shoulders are slumped. He looks upset. Her eyebrows are scrunched. She looks angry.* Make facial expressions in the mirror: *let's look silly! Let's make a happy face.* After a big emotion or a tantrum or meltdown, ask them how they felt

right before they exploded/fell apart. A list of examples is coming up in "The Signs."

2. *You have big feelings. I do too:* Model handling your big emotions with calmness and composure. You can either model this intentionally or unintentionally, but whatever you do to handle frustration, your kids are going to be watching and learning. Try to learn your triggers and pay attention to the clues your body gives you, and use the same strategies that you would like to teach your kids. Of course, every person is different. Not all strategies will work for you or your kids. You'll probably have to try multiple to determine which ones are the best for the both of you. For example, if you accidentally spill your cup of coffee on your jeans before getting in the car, you could either scream and curse and throw a fit, or you could take a deep breath, and say, "Ugh.

I'm so frustrated. We were ready to go, and now I have to make a new cup of coffee and get dressed again. I am going to splash some cold water on my wrists to calm down and then put on my back up outfit." Either way, your kids will learn something.

There are even times where it might make sense to manufacture a behavior modeling situation. Maybe your child has been struggling to stay calm when they are told to get dressed for the day. You could narrate your emotions one morning explaining how frustrated you are to have to get dressed and leave the house, model taking deep breaths or repeating a mantra, and then remind yourself (out loud) why it's important to do boring things sometimes.

I wouldn't recommend using a forced modeling situation often because your child may start to sense inauthenticity. Sometimes, it's a great way for them to see you work through something similar to what they are going through though.

3. *I'll show you what I do to make it through:* Here's where you will explicitly teach calm-down strategies to your child. It's not enough, and honestly it's not recommended, to just tell your child to "take a deep breath" while they are experiencing a big emotion. That's the equivalent of someone telling you to "calm down" when you're mad. Instead, while they are calm, say something like, "You know how sometimes you get mad/sad/frustrated/embarrassed? I'd love to show you some ways I handle those big feelings. Is now or after dinner a good time?" And then act them out together. You show them

how you do it, and let them show you. A list of ideas is coming up in "The Strategies."

4. *And prove that I'll be here for you:* More than anything, our kids want to know they are loved by us. Proving to your child that they are safe to show their big emotions to you without you dismissing, ignoring, shaming, scolding, or shushing them will go a long way toward helping them work through their feelings. They will know that no matter what, they have a safe place to land when they fall. We, as parents, can also "lend" our emotional regulation to our kids when they are in a meltdown. If we are able to stay calm and model that calmness, they may instinctively copy us. If we are able to give them a hug, our touch, our breathing, and our heartbeats might give them a sense of calm too.

The Signs:

Depending on the emotion, our bodies will give us lots of clues to prepare us for their arrival. Being able to identify them early is key to helping us emotionally regulate in the moment so that we can work through them more effectively later. Some of the physiological responses overlap, so it can be difficult to know exactly what's coming. Honestly, though, we frequently have more than one feeling at a time, and knowing how to regulate during one emotion can usually help regulate through the others as well. Here are some of the most common physiological responses to some of the most common big emotions. Try to make a list of the ones that are common for you and your child.

Common Physiological Responses to Emotions

Angry	Racing/pounding heart, tight muscles, red face, clenched hands, clenched jaw, rapid breathing, furrowed eyebrows, heavy breathing, increased body temperature, sweating, stomachache, clouded thinking, focused thinking
Sad	Crying/teary eyes, racing/pounding heart, tight muscles, fast/heavy breathing, tight chest, chest pains, stomachache, clouded thinking, change in appetite
Nervous	Headache, nausea, racing/pounding heart, chest pain, dizziness, twitching, sweating, inability to sit still, fatigue, insomnia, stomachaches, "butterflies" in stomach, increased urination
Embarrassed	Racing/pounding heart, blushing, looking at ground, rapid breathing, stuttering, tied tongue, dilated pupils, stomachache
Happy	Smiling mouth, increased/decreased heart rate, relaxed body, buzzing feeling, "butterflies" in stomach, glowing sking, clear thinking, improved digestion

The Strategies:

The Strategy	How to do it
Deep Breaths	Try box breathing: Breathe in for 4 counts, hold for 4 counts, exhale for 4 counts, hold for 4 counts. Repeat x4
Squeeze or fidget with Something	Clench and unclench your fists while you take deep breaths. Squeeze a stress ball or a squishy toy. Play with a fidget.
Rocket ship	Wrap your arms around yourself like a hug. Squeeze and inhale. Hold as your countdown from 5. After you countdown, exhale and let your arms point to the sky like a rocket.
Calm down cream	Pick a scented lotion that you enjoy- lavender, mint, and vanilla are calming. Squirt some into your hands and rub them together. Smell the

	lotion in a deep breath. Gently pull each finger and "throw away" the anger as you get to the fingertip.
Glitter jar	Search for glitter jars or sensory jars online. You can either build one or purchase one. Swirl the items and watch them slowly fall down.
Count back from 5	Count backwards as you take deep breaths
Write about it	Write down what happened. Let your pen flow freely and do not stop until you have gotten it all out. You can also set a timer for 10 minutes and ask yourself to write until it stops.
Draw it	Draw what happened. You can also draw a potential solution or what you wish would have happened.

Act it out	Role play with another person or toys. Talk about how you felt when certain things happened. Act out different endings. Talk about how those make you feel.
Read	Take yourself out of the moment with a good book. Distract yourself until you are ready to process. Or read a book about a similar situation to see how someone else handled it.
Repeat a Mantra	Pick something you can say for every situation or for each individual one. Check the Songs & Mantras chapter for some examples.
Look at photos	Keep a photo album or a photo wall in your calm down corner. Have pictures of people and places that you love and that make you feel safe.
Sort	Get a bag of different kinds of beans, pasta,

something	pebbles, etc. Use separate bowls or a bowl with different sections to sort them out. Giving your hands something repetitive to do might get your brain to start thinking of solutions.
Hug a friend/pet	Hugging our kids (if they allow it) during big emotions is HUGE. It shows them we love them even when they are upset. And physical touch; when welcome, is a big stress reliever.
Hug a stuffed animal	You can hug them, wipe your tears on them, twirl their tails, rub their tags- lots of calming sensations.
Talk to yourself	Walk around, pace, or do something mindless with your body while you talk yourself through your problem.
Talk to a	If you are able to; call, text, or face-to-face talk

149

friend	with a friend or family member.
Butterfly taps	Cross your arms over your chest. Take turns lightly tapping either side as you take slow, deep breaths.
Rub your earlobes	Rub each ear with the hand on the opposite side of your body starting at the lobe and moving up slowly.
Hum a low note	Hold one low note as long as you can.
Walk away	Leave the room for a few minutes. If you are with another person, say, "I need a break. I'll be back."
Splash water on your face	Splash cold water on your face. Look at yourself in the mirror if there is one available. Remind yourself that you can handle this.
Run cold	Pick one wrist or both and let cool water run over

water on your wrist	it.
Put your face somewhere cool	Open the refrigerator to let cool air hit your face, stand near a fan to let it blow on you, or lay your face on a cool surface like a countertop.
Midline Cross Self-hug	This one is tricky to write. Hold your arms out in front of you. Pretend you are going to clap your hands together, but let them pass each other. Once your arms are crossed at the wrist, rotate your wrists so that your palms face down. Then, continue to rotate them inward, so that you can hold hands with yourself. Bring your clasped hands under your arms and up against your chest. You can also cross your legs and ankles. Take deep breaths. This pose is great lying down as

		well.
Go somewhere dark and quiet		Find a room without too much noise. Turn the lights off and sit still for a while. Reduce external stimulation.
Do Yoga		Find a yoga video on YouTube, or simply sit criss-cross with your hands on your knees and eyes closed.
Take a shower		Let the water wash over you. Cry if you need to. Talk to yourself if you need to. The shower is the ultimate calm down spot, in my opinion.

Chapter 18

Songs & Mantras

LINKS

(Ways to Link or Connect With Your Kids)

To the tune of "Old MacDonald Had a Farm"

The Lyrics:

Love on them in many ways

(L-I-N-K-S)

Immerse yourself in chat or play

(L-I-N-K-S)

Notice things your hear or see

(L-I-N-K-S)

Know and respect their boundaries

(L-I-N-K-S)

Show up when they need you to

(That's how you connect)

The Thought Process:

It might feel like we are wrapping things up, but this should have been the first chapter. One of my favorite quotes is from John C. Maxwell who said, "Students [or kids] don't care how much you know until they know how much you care." We HAVE to connect with our kids before they will listen to us. Building relationships with our kids is not only something that will bring us great joy, but it will also encourage them to listen, collaborate with you, and follow directions when necessary.

"Expectations – The 8C Method"

The Lyrics:

(To the tune of Frere Jacques)

Take a deep breath

Move in close next

Be direct

What do you expect?

Give short tasks or give a choice

A consequence you can enforce

See what they do

And follow through

The Thought Process:

      This is basically the song version of the CCCCCCCC or 8C method. I just wrote it to help you remember the steps. Go back to that chapter for a more in-depth discussion

"The Grounding Song"

(A way to remember a grounding exercise during panic attacks)

The Lyrics

Get grounded with me

Find 5 things you can see

Now 4 things you can feel

Touch them all for real

3 things that you hear

You're doing great, my dear

2 things you can smell

You're doing very well

Now we're almost done

We're here at number 1

Say 1 thing that you know

Because I love you so

The Thought Process

The 54321 method for grounding has a few variations. It might be hard for your child to remember what to do for each number; and the last thing anyone needs while panicking is more stress. It's like trying to remember which wire to cut on the bomb. (It's the red one. No, the white. Definitely red. See?) I thought a song might be easier for kids to remember. And bonus, it's a soft soothing melody. I can't share that with you on paper, but I'll try to sing it on the audiobook or have it available on YouTube or social media soon.

MANTRAS

Here are some ideas to repeat in your head when you are trying to emotionally regulate yourself during your child's big emotions:

He's not giving me a hard time. He's having a hard time.

He needs my help.

This too will pass.

I can do this.

She is a child. I am an adult.

I have the tools to handle this.

I need to be curious.

I set the tone.

My goal is to connect.

The most important thing here is our relationship.

She has an unmet need.

All emotions are okay.

I can only control my reactions.

We will learn from this.

Her behavior is not a reflection of my parenting.

He is allowed to be upset.

I am choosing to bring calm.

This feels like an emergency, but it is not.

Deep breaths.

Chapter 19

Resources and Recommendations

Places to Learn More

Books:

There are thousands of books that would help you on this journey, but I am only going to recommend the ones I have actually read (or completed at least 75%. I have ADHD. Books are hard for me sometimes):

No Drama Discipline by Tina Payne Bryson PhD., and Daniel J. Siegel M.D.

The Explosive Child by Dr. Ross W. Greene

Gentle Discipline by Sarah Ockwell Smith

What Happened to You by Bruce D. Perry, MD, PhD and Oprah Winfrey

Teaching with Love and Logic by Jim Fay and David Funk*

<u>Conscious Discipline</u> by Dr. Becky A. Bailey

<u>Managing Emotional Mayhem</u> by Dr. Becky A. Bailey

*Although this book is for teachers, there is another book for parents.

Programs:

Conscious Discipline

CHAMPS

Love and Logic

Capturing Kids Hearts

Podcasts:

Good Inside with Dr. Becky

Respectful Parenting: Janet Lansbury

Raising Good Humans

Social Media:

Instagram

@kindminds_smarthearts

@drbeckywithgoodinside

@destini.ann

@mrchazz

Tiktok

@the_indomitable_blackman

@toriphantom

@twomorayeels

@theconsideratemomma

@highimpactclub

@domesticblisters

@lesleypsyd

References

Amy Morin, L. C. S. W. (2022, August 9). *4 types of parenting styles and their effects on kids*. Verywell Family. Retrieved February 23, 2023, from https://www.verywellfamily.com/types-of-parenting-styles-1095045

Anderson, J. (2021, April 13). *The effect of spanking on the brain*. Harvard Graduate School of Education. Retrieved February 23, 2023, from https://www.gse.harvard.edu/news/uk/21/04/effect-spanking-brain

Central, C. A. O., Churchill, A., Tyner, A., & Pondiscio, R. (2021, April 8). *Children learn best when they feel safe and valued*. The Thomas B. Fordham Institute. Retrieved February 23, 2023, from https://fordhaminstitute.org/national/commentary/children-learn-best-when-they-feel-safe-and-valued

Howard, J. (2018, March 13). *These are the countries where spanking is illegal*. CNN. Retrieved February 23, 2023, from https://www.cnn.com/2018/03/12/health/spanking-laws-parenting-without-borders-intl/index.html

Mullins, J. L., & Tashjian, S. M. (2018, May 16). *Parenting Styles and Child Behavior*. Psychology in action. Retrieved February 23, 2023, from https://www.psychologyinaction.org/?s=parenting%2Bstyles

Social Worker. The Sims Wiki. (n.d.). Retrieved February 23, 2023, from https://sims.fandom.com/wiki/Social_worker

Team, T. T. P. (2022, November 29). *Natural versus logical consequences*. Parenting Now. Retrieved February 23, 2023, from https://parentingnow.org/natural-versus-logical-consequences/

Acknowledgements

Thank you to my husband, Luciano, for being patient with me, believing in me, and giving me the time and space to create. I will never forget your confidence in me.

Thank you to my son, Max, for saving my life. You make me want to be the best person I can be, and you make me smile every day. I am forever grateful for the chance to know you and love you.

Thank you to my mom, Barbara, who is now a moth. Moths can't read, so this is probably a waste of book space. I'll light a candle for you. Thank you for loving me and being my number one fan. You did the best you could.

Thank you to my dad, Clive, for always making sure I had what I needed. And thank you for the moments when the walls came down. Our times together have been too few, but they have been very meaningful.

Thank you to my brother, Bryce, for making me laugh through everything. You are the funniest person I know. I miss you, so I'll start a podcast for us soon.

Thank you to my sister, Rowena, for being an example of who I want to be when I grow up.

Thank you to my step-mom, Michelle, for being so understanding of me when I screw up and giving such solid advice before I do.

Thank you to my sissy-in-law, Sarah, for being the most amazing travel partner, goss listener, and shirt-tucker-reminder on the planet. And ALSO thank you for helping me so incredibly often with your impeccable design skills.

Thank you to my best friend, Coco, for being my hype-lady and idea bouncer-offerer.

Thank you to my friends and family for smiling and nodding every time I talked about my Tiktoks, or gentle parenting, or my book.

Thank you to my former bosses: Helen Welk, Kelly Mitchell, Kimberly Toney, Victoria Kwan, Mary Anne Bronson, Ryan Pavone, Tammy Hinton, and Ricardo Marquez for pointing out that I needed to improve my knowledge of child development and sending me to trainings.

Thank you to Jackie and Karen for your very sweet testimonials and general good vibes. You are both so kind and supportive.

Thank you to my social media mommy family. I'm scared to start listing names because I will certainly accidentally leave someone out and that would make me feel so horrible. BUT y'all have been my everything the last few years. Internet friends are for real.

Find out more about Jackie and her work:

Email: jackie@kindmindssmarthearts.com

Tiktok: @kindminds_smarthearts
Instagram: @kindminds_smarthearts
Facebook: @kindminds_smarthearts
Twitter: @kindminds_

Made in the USA
Middletown, DE
30 July 2023